TIM JEFFS ART
Animal Sketches
Sea Life

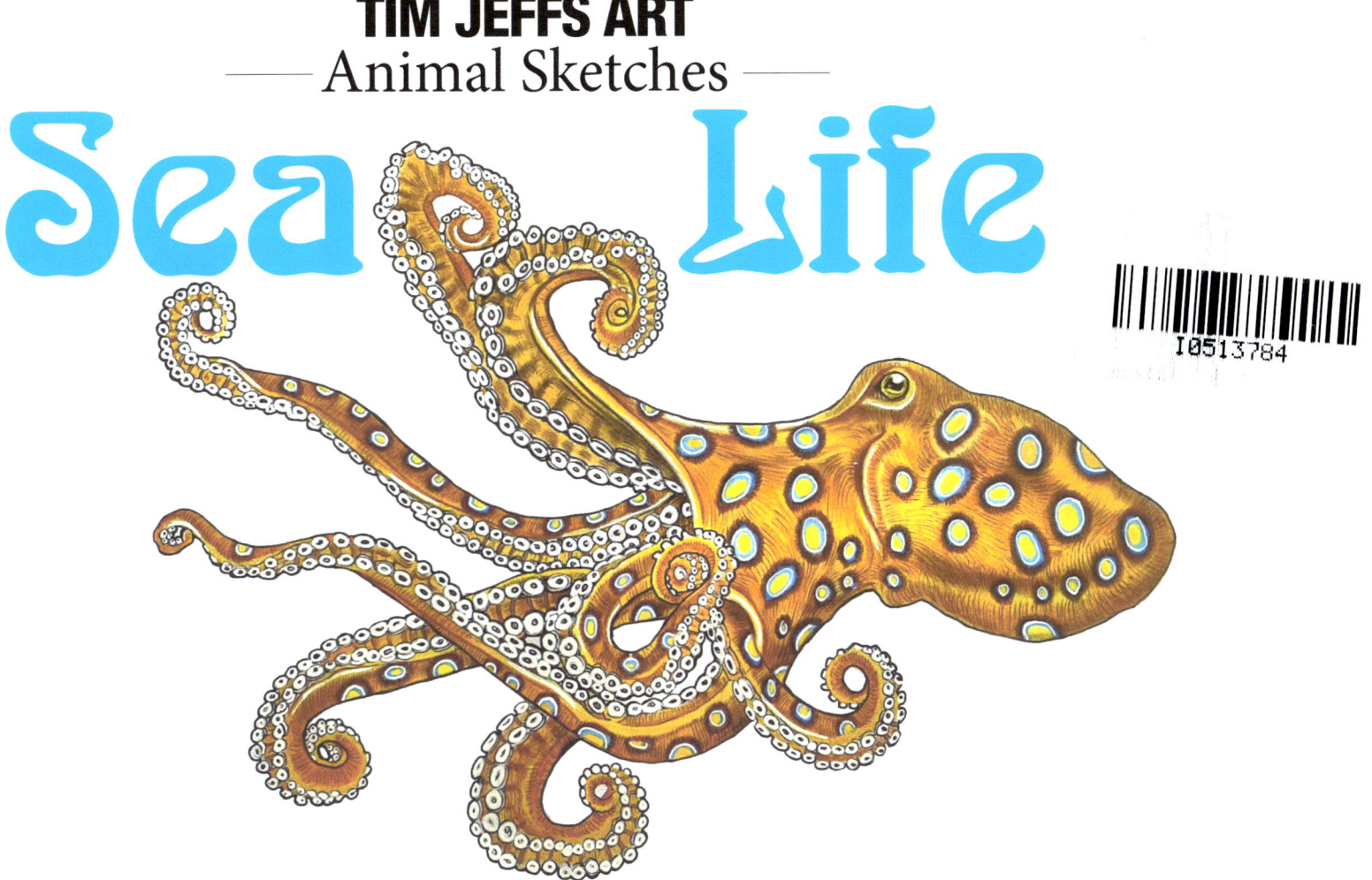

A Special Edition Coloring Book

For Jane, Jenna and Harrison

Dedicated to all of the wonderful colorists who have supported my art and made my drawings
more beautiful with their colors, and all the precious creatures that we live among.
A special thank you to Jo Warren for all of her continued support and beautiful colorings
and lesson that make this book so much more special!

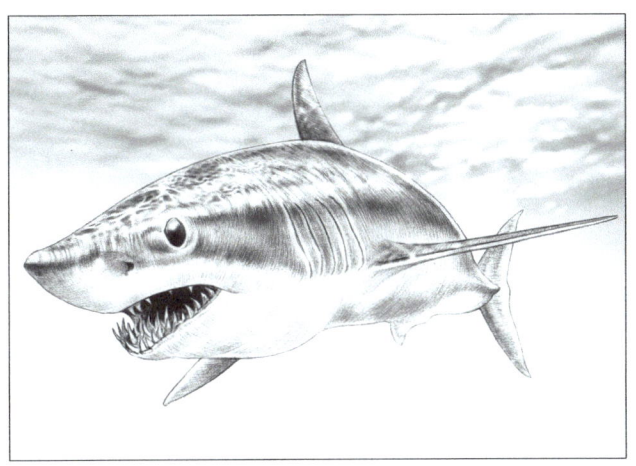 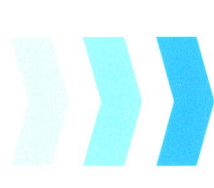 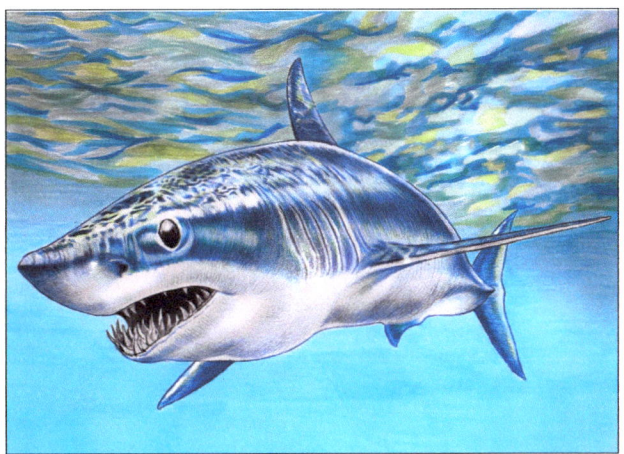

© Copyright 2021 Tim Jeffs Art
All rights reserved. No part of this publication may be reproduced or
distributed in any form without the prior written permission of Tim Jeffs Art.

Tim Jeffs Art
376 East Madison Avenue, Dumont, NJ 07628

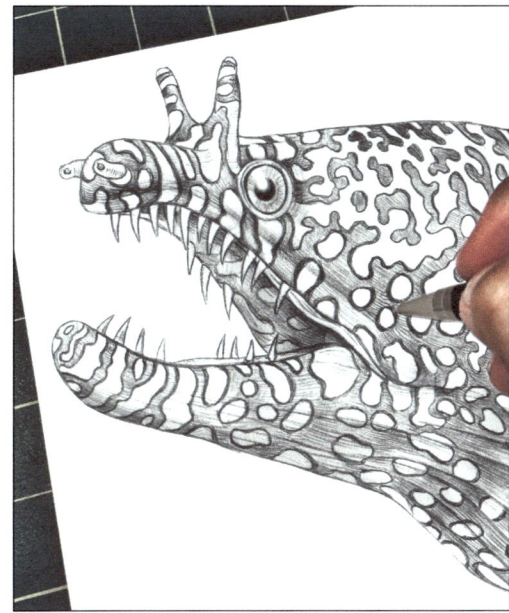 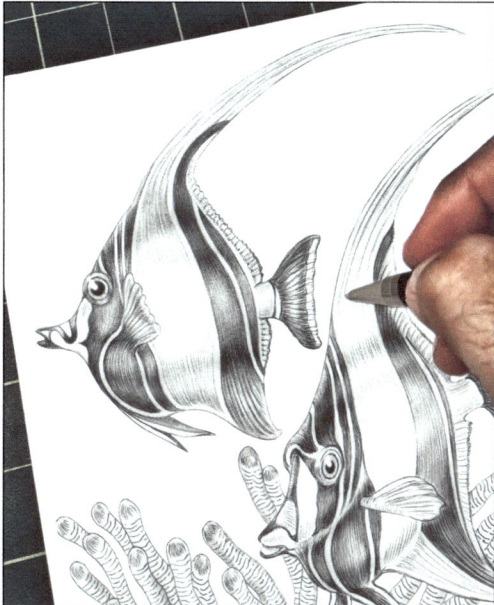 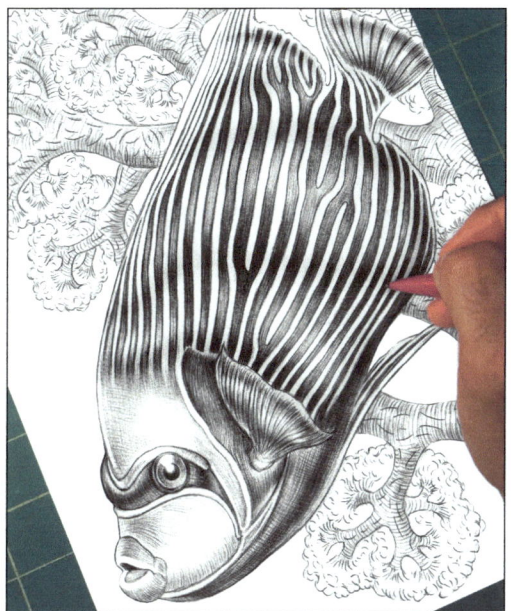

Sea Life Sketches Thoughts

I highly recommend experiencing snorkeling or scuba diving in the ocean if you haven't already.
I will never forget the first time I put on a scuba diving mask and jumped into the ocean on a coral reef. It was like entering an alien world filled with the most beautiful and colorful creatures. My brother and I were just teenagers at the time and after our first dive we couldn't get enough of "getting wet" as divers call it. On every dive we experienced new forms of life. From endless varieties of fish, to sea turtles, crustaceans, Moray eels, dolphins, sharks and we were even lucky enough to dive among whales. Water covers 75 percent of our planet and I firmly believe every one, if able, should see with their own eyes the fascinating water world that this planet has.

In some of the drawings in this coloring book I have included the ocean creatures in their underwater environments. May this give you further coloring creativity options to have fun with.

I hope you enjoy coloring this group of sea life sketches as much as I enjoyed drawing them, and I know that with your colors, you will bring these amazing creatures and their undersea world to life!

GRAYSCALE COLORING LESSON
Clown Triggerfish

Moderate

Coloring the Clown Triggerfish

On the next page I will walk you through the coloring of the Clown Triggerfish which is on page 2 of this coloring book. I was able to see these strikingly beautiful fish on coral reefs in the wild while scuba diving in Micronesia in the South Pacific. This beautiful coloring of the Clown Triggerfish was done by Jo Warren. Many thanks for her creative and inspirational step-by-step photos in the coloring lesson.

❯ Supply List

In this lesson, Faber Castell Polychromos pencils were used, (pencil numbers are listed below) but you can use any brand with similar colors.

1) **The coloring page can be found on page 2**
2) **Colors: Faber Castell Polychromos pencils:**
   - 101 White
   - 102 Cream
   - 106 Light Chrome Yellow
   - 107 Cadmium Yellow
   - 110 Phthalo Blue
   - 111 Cadmium Orange
   - 113 Orange Glaze
   - 117 Light Cadmium Red
   - 151 Helio Blue-Reddish
   - 167 Permanent Green Olive
   - 180 Raw Umber
   - 219 Scarlet Red
   - 266 Permanent Green

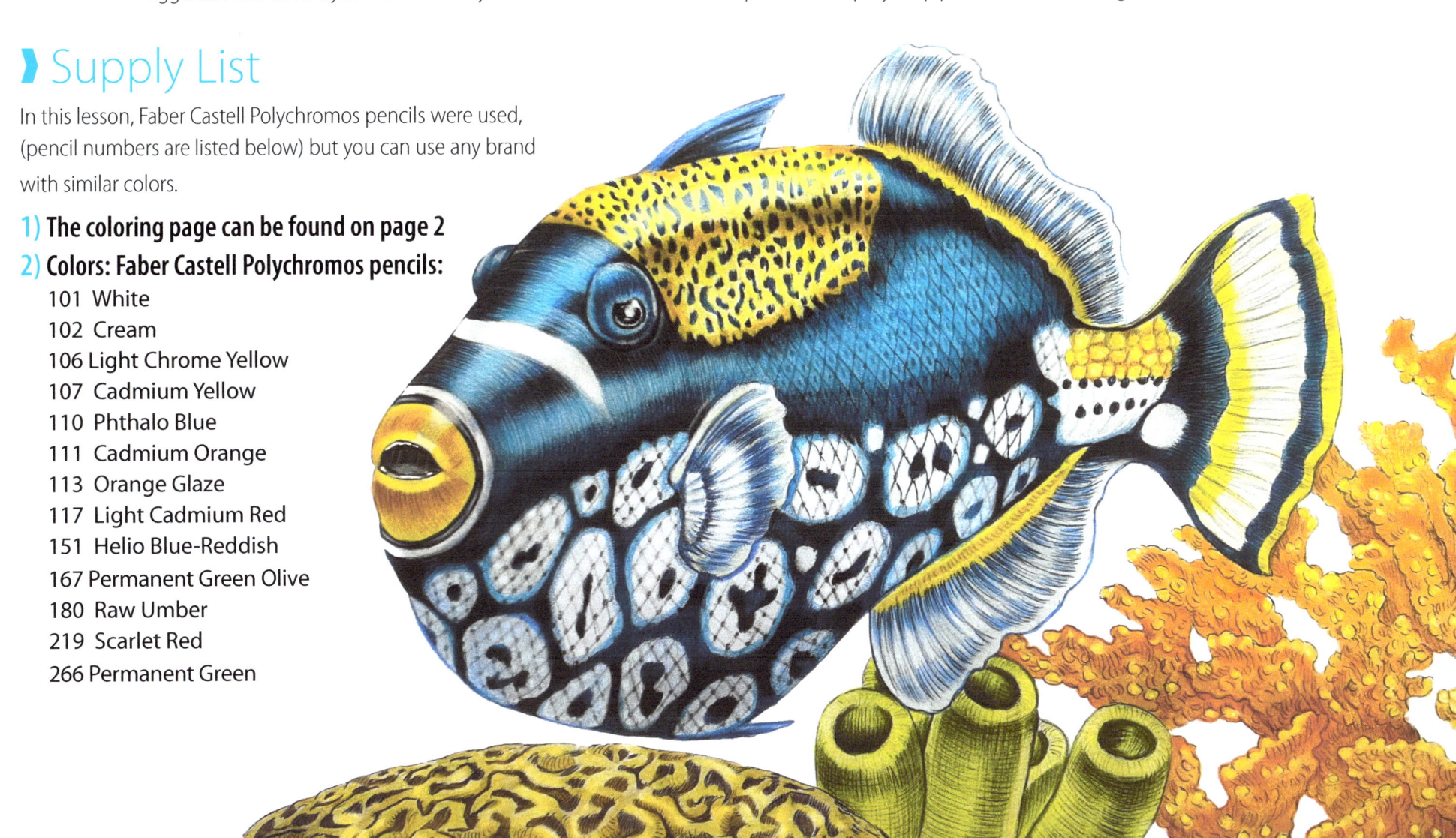

GRAYSCALE COLORING LESSON
Clown Triggerfish

Clown Triggerfish
Supplies needed: A variety of colorful pencils

You did it! Your Clown Triggerfish is done! Coloring Steps by Jo Warren

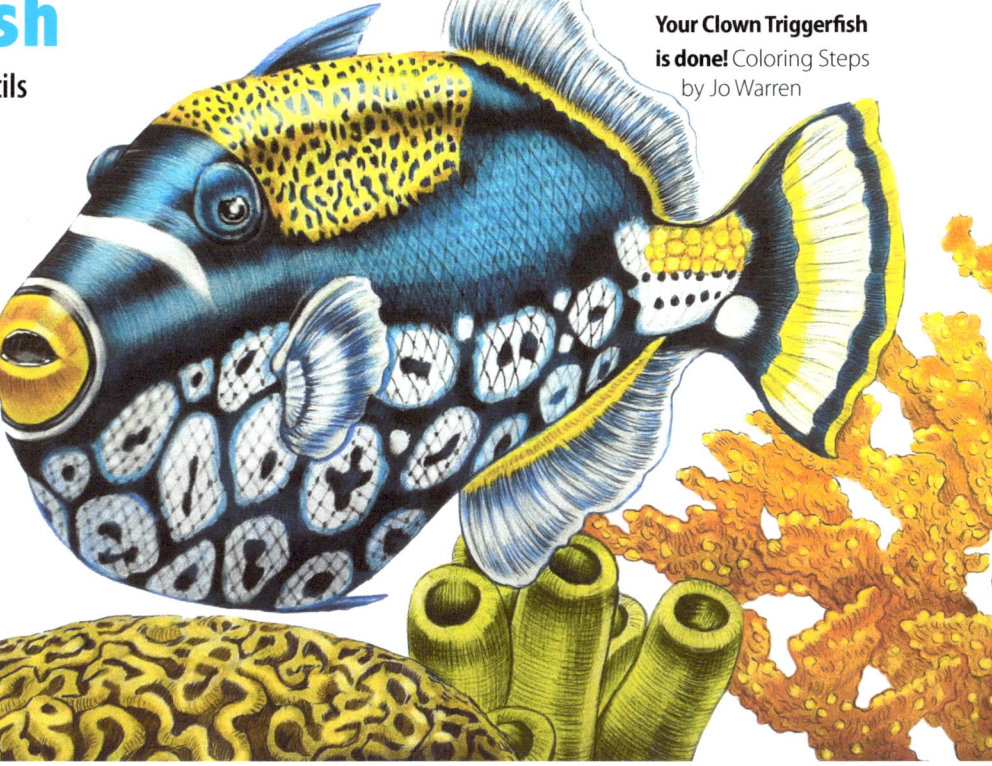

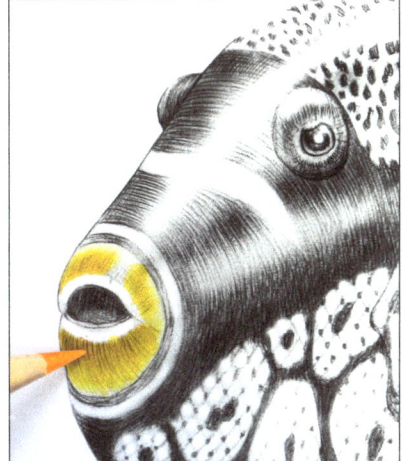

Step 1. Color the area around the mouth first with Cadmium Yellow (107). Then layer Cadmium Orange (111) on top of the yellow, but not over the lips and the outer edge of the yellow ring.

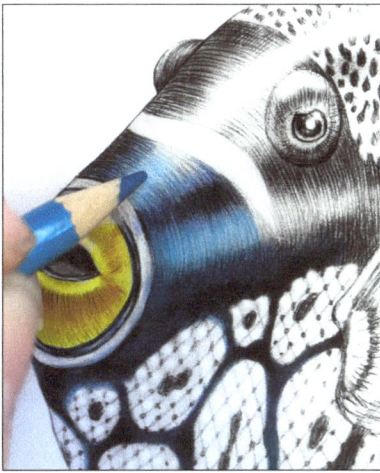

Step 2. To achieve the shiny look of the fish's scales color a base coat of White (101) over the light areas. Then color Phthalo Blue (110) over the light and dark areas. Finally layer Helioblue-Reddish (151) over the dark areas.

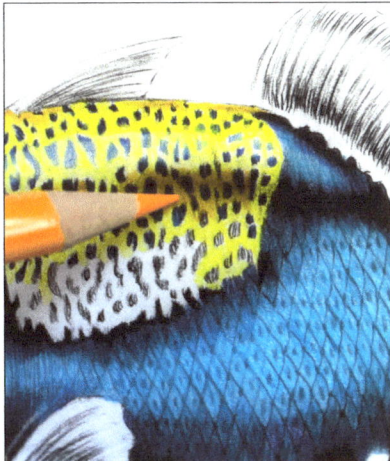

Step 3. Color Cadmium Yellow (107) over the spotted area on the back. Then color in the spots with Phthalo Blue (110). To create the shadow area on the back color in the shaded stripe with Cadmium Orange (111).

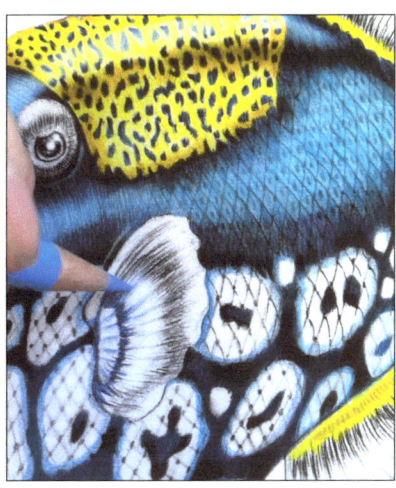

Step 4. First color a base of White (101) on the body spots.. Then outline the spots by edging them with Light Phthalo Blue (145). Use the same color to shade in the dark areas of the pectoral fin.

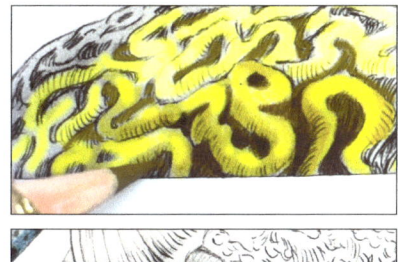
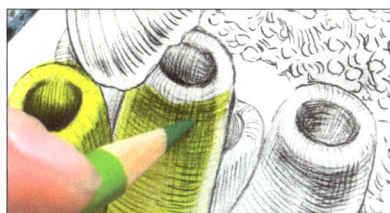

Step 5. For the left side brain coral color the dark areas with Raw Umber (180). Color the lighter areas first with Cream (102) and then layer Light Cadmium Yellow on top. For the center coral tubes start with Permanent Green (266) and use Permanent Green Olive (167) for the darker areas.

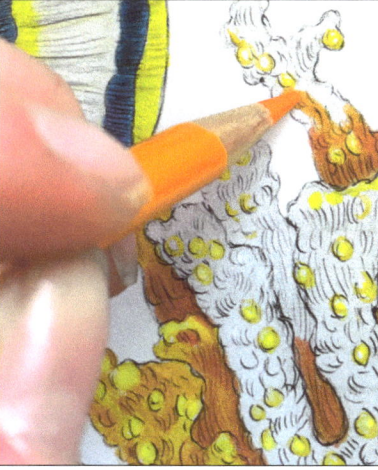

Step 6. Color in the dots of the coral with Light Chrome Yellow (106). Color in the rest of the coral using Orange Glaze (113). To achieve the darker areas layer Light Cadmium Red (117) and finally Scarlet Red on top (219).

Spreading Awareness through Coloring

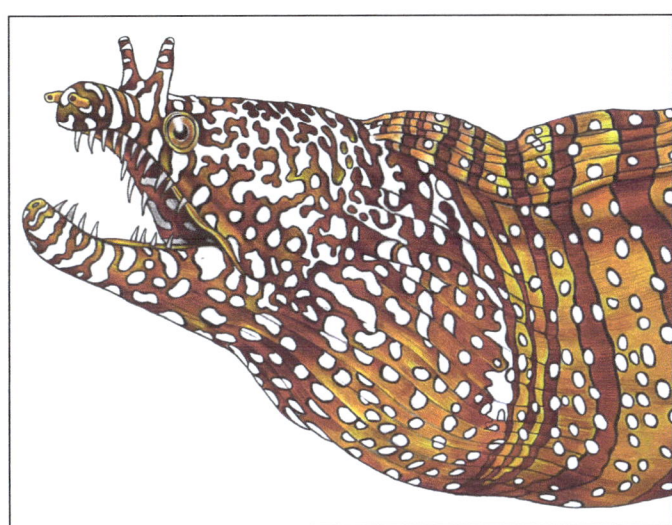

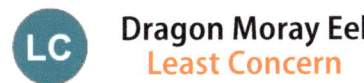 **Dragon Moray Eel**
Least Concern

I truly believe that raising awareness through the sharing of my artwork is a fantastic way to educate people about conservation. And coloring animals is a beautiful way to learn about them as you enjoy a relaxing and fun pastime. On the following page, I listed the Sea Creatures statuses on the *International Union for Conservation of Nature's (IUCN)* conservation list. I think it's important to include the *(IUCN)* conservation list so people understand the classifications more clearly. To the right is an overview of the IUCN's conservation list, which breaks animals' conservation statuses into several categories. Knowing what these categories mean and the animals that are included in them is extremely important. **Together through art we can change the world!**

Tim Jeffs
Animal Artist

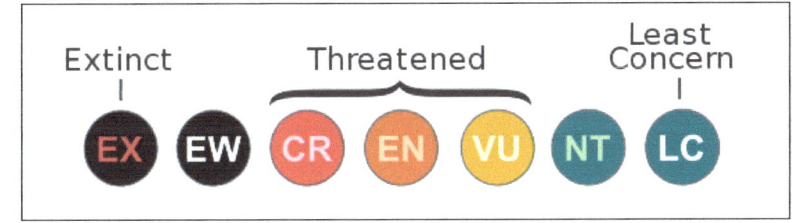

The list consists of 7 categories. From Least Concerned all the way to Extinct. Here are the definitions of each category:

- **LEAST CONCERN (LC):** A species that has been evaluated but not qualified for any other category on the list.
- **NEAR THREATENED (NT):** A species that may be considered threatened with extinction in the near future.
- **VULNERABLE (VU):** A species likely to become endangered unless the circumstances that are threatening its survival and reproduction improve.
- **ENDANGERED (EN):** A species that is considered very likely to become extinct.
- **CRITICALLY ENDANGERED (CR):** A species that is facing an extremely high risk of becoming extinct in the wild.
- **EXTINCT IN THE WILD (EW):** A species that is only known by living members kept in captivity or as a naturalized population outside its historic range due to massive habitat loss.
- **EXTINCT (EX):** A species that has been terminated.

Learn about the Sea Life

Before you start coloring, it's important to learn where the sea life in this book lives and to know its conservation status.

❱ Blue Ringed Octopus
Found in the Pacific and Indian oceans from Japan to Australia, they are recognized as one of the world's most venomous marine animals.
Conservation Status: Least Concern

❱ Clown Triggerfish
Widely distributed in the waters of the Indian Ocean, western Pacific Ocean and the western Atlantic Ocean. This fish has become tame enough to be hand-fed.
Conservation Status: Least Concern

❱ Dragon Moray Eel
Widespread throughout the Indo-Pacific oceans it grows up to 92 cm in length and lives in rocky reefs.
Conservation Status: Least Concern

❱ Emperor Angelfish
Stable in population this fish faces no major threats of extinction. They are found on reefs in the Indian Ocean, Pacific Ocean and Red Sea.
Conservation Status: Least Concern

❱ Giant Squid
Growing to the tremendous size of 59 feet the first images of a Giant Squid in it's natural habitat were taken in 2004.
Conservation Status: Least Concern

❱ Great Barracuda
Living in the Indian, Pacific and Atlantic oceans these fish are found from mangrove areas to deep reefs. Though they are not threatened yet, Florida is considering imposing catch limits.
Conservation Status: Least Concern

❱ Great Hammerhead Shark
Growing to a maximum length of 20 feet, they can be found in tropical and warm waters worldwide. Over fishing has made them extremely vulnerable and considered critically endangered.
Conservation Status: Critically Endangered

❱ Hawksbill Sea Turtle
Found in oceans worldwide they grow to an average size of 180 lb. It gets it's name from it's curved, pointed beak, which resembles that of a bird of prey. They are threatened due to pollution and loss of nesting areas.
Conservation Status: Critically Endangered

❱ Humpback Whale
A baleen whale the Humpback Whale grows to a length of 52 feet. Found in oceans and seas around the world. It was once hunted to the brink of extinction until a 1966 moratorium.
Conservation Status: Least Concern

❱ Map Pufferfish
Found in tropical and subtropical waters from the Indian Ocean to the western Pacific Ocean They contain an extremely toxic sodium channel blocker which protects it from predators.
Conservation Status: Least Concern

❱ Moorish Idol
Widely distributed throughout the Indo-Pacific they were named by the Moors of Africa who believed the fish to be a bringer of happiness.
Conservation Status: Least Concern

❱ Orcas
The largest member of the toothed whales Orcas are found in each of the world's oceans. They live in highly social family groups. In 2018 the global populations were found to be in dramatic decline due to pollution.
Conservation Status: Endangered

❱ Regal Blue Tang
Living throughout the Indo-Pacific, Regal Blue Tangs are one of the most popular marine aquarium fish all around the world.
Conservation Status: Least Concern

❱ Shortfin Mako Shark
Reaching lengths up to 13 feet and weighing 2200 pounds they are one of the fastest sharks swimming up to 45 miles per hour. They are threatened by both sport and commercial fisheries.
Conservation Status: Endangered

❱ Swordfish
Distributed widely in tropical and temperate parts of the Atlantic, Pacific, and Indian Ocean they can grow up to 15 feet in length. Through protection their numbers have been stabilized.
Conservation Status: Least Concern

Sea Life Index

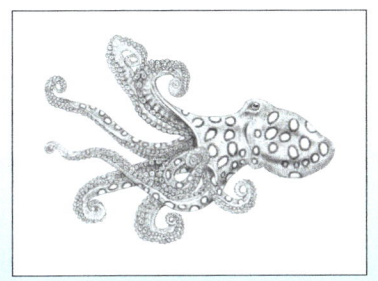
Blue Ringed Octopus 1

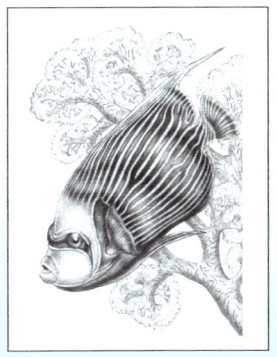
Emperor Angelfish 4

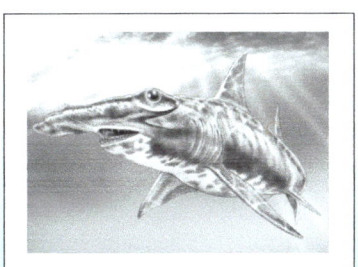
Great Hammerhead Shark 7

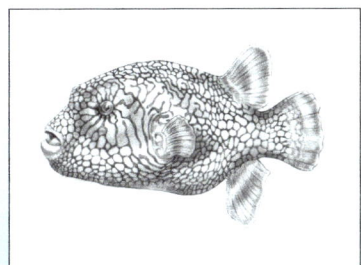
Map Pufferfish 10

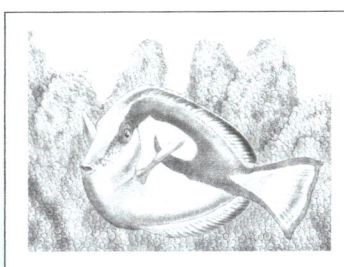
Regal Blue Tang 13

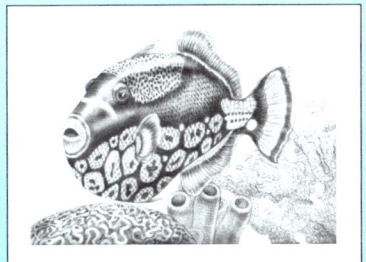
Clown Triggerfish 2

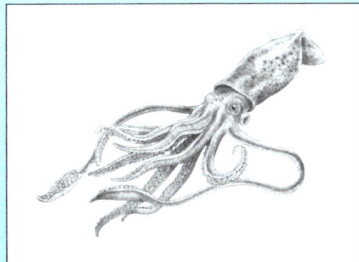
Giant Squid 5

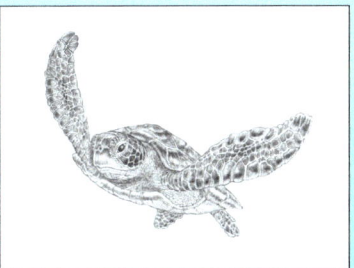
Hawksbill Sea Turtle 8

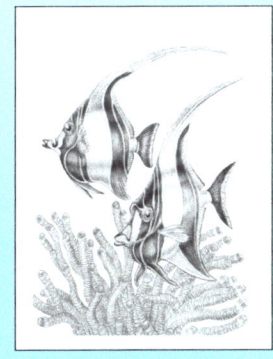
Moorish Idol 11

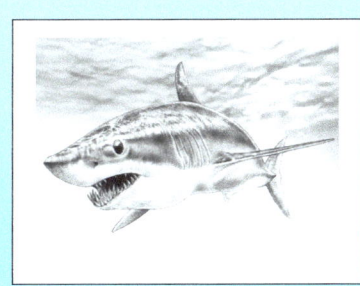
Shortfin Mako Shark 14

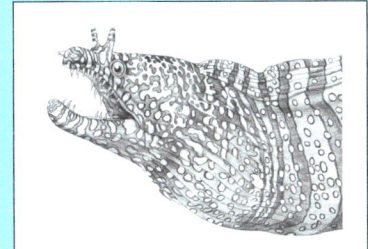
Dragon Moray Eel 3

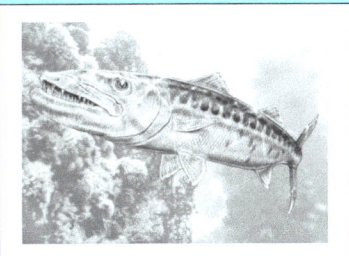
Great Barracuda 6

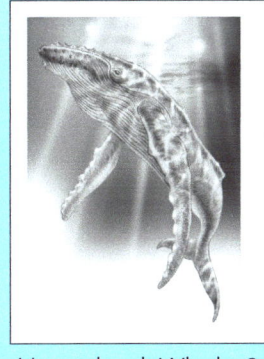
Humpback Whale 9

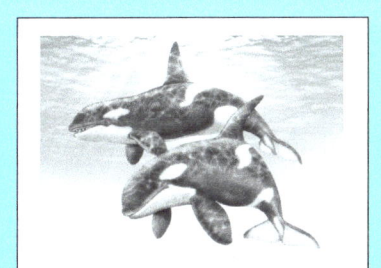
Orcas 12

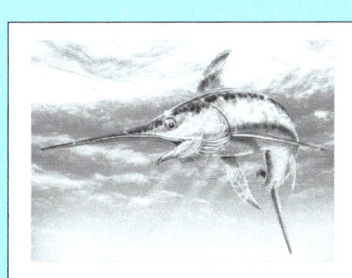
Swordfish 15

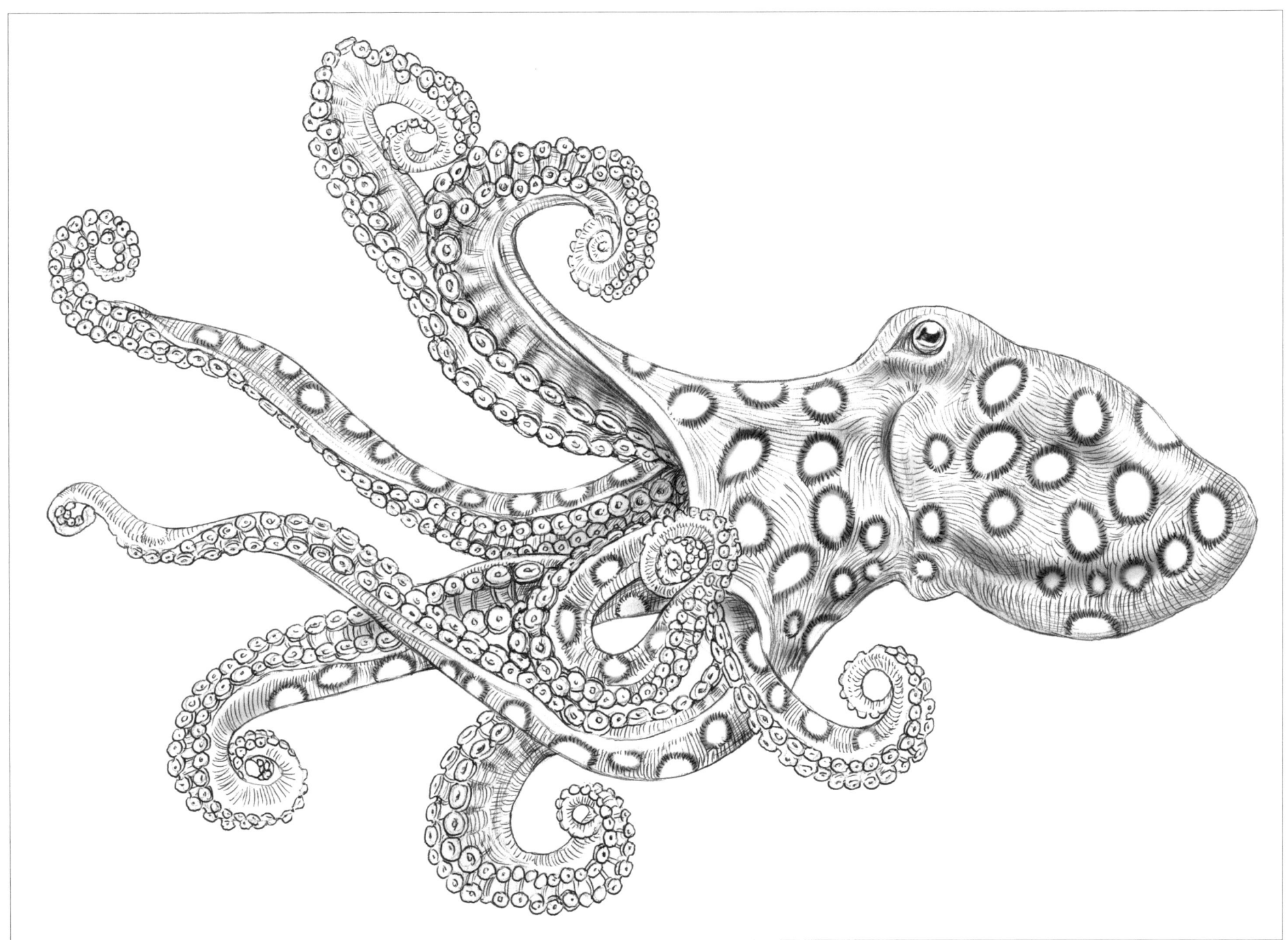

Blue-Ringed Octopus

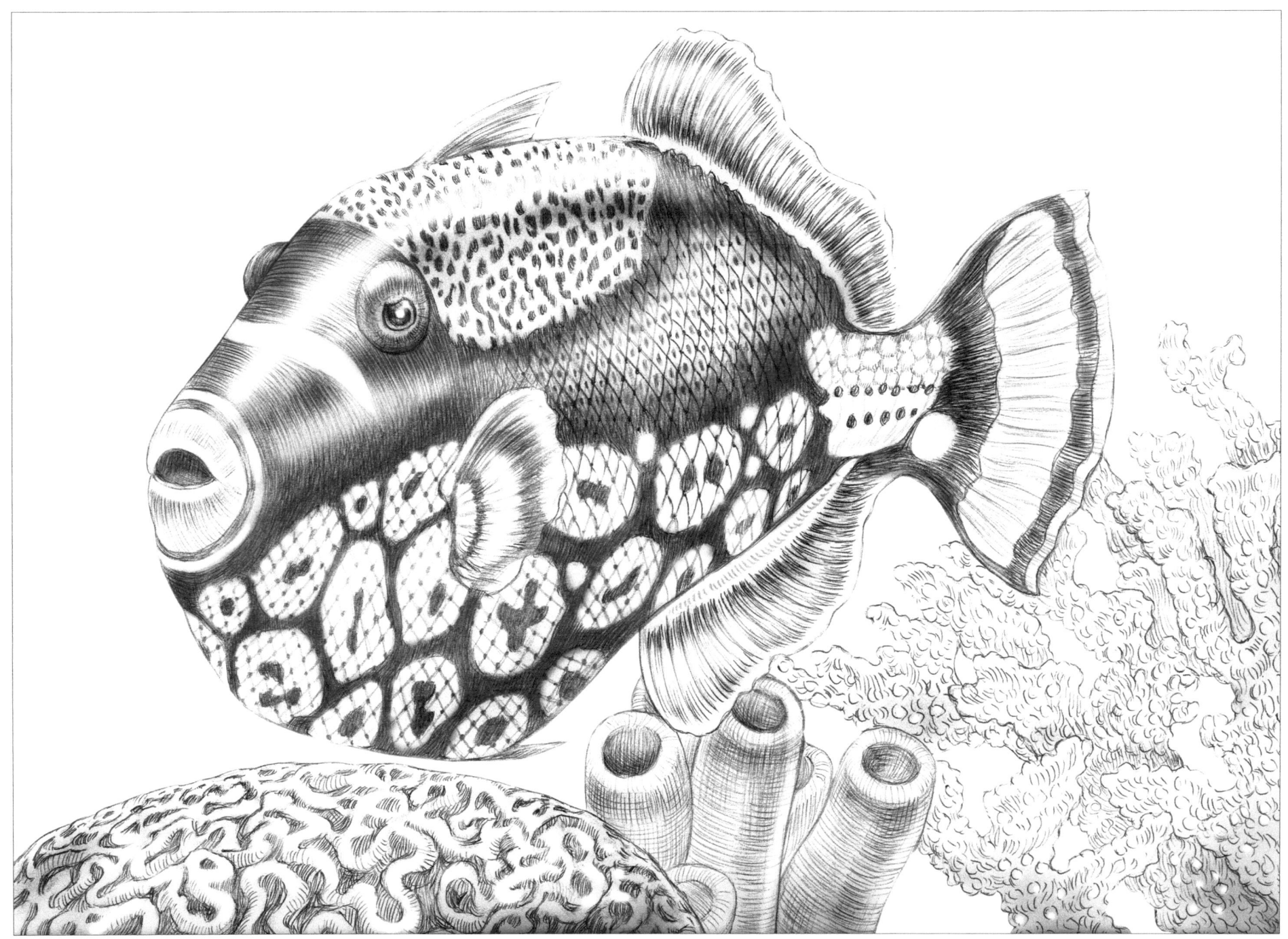

Clown Triggerfish

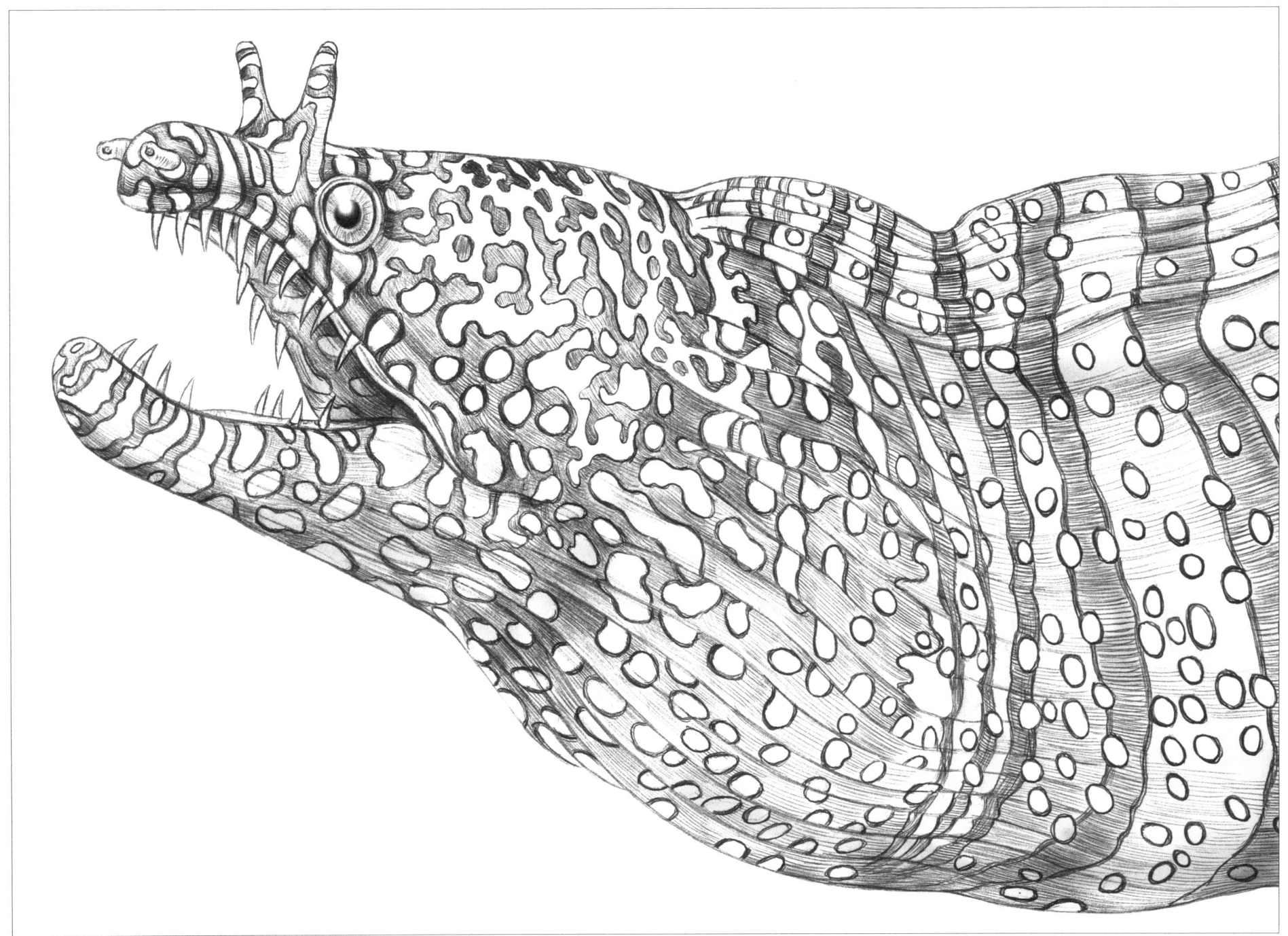

Dragon Moray Eel

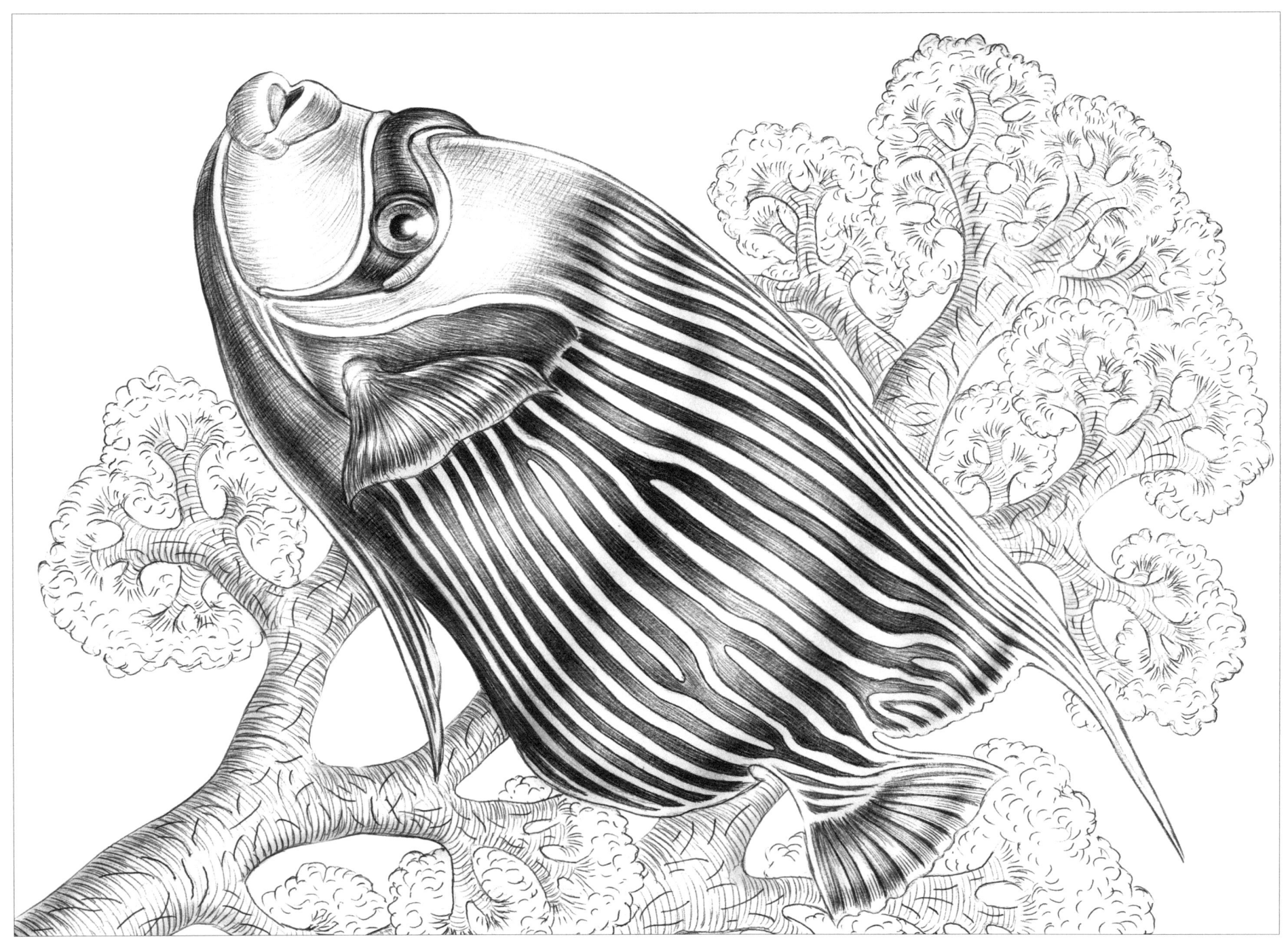

Emperor Angelfish

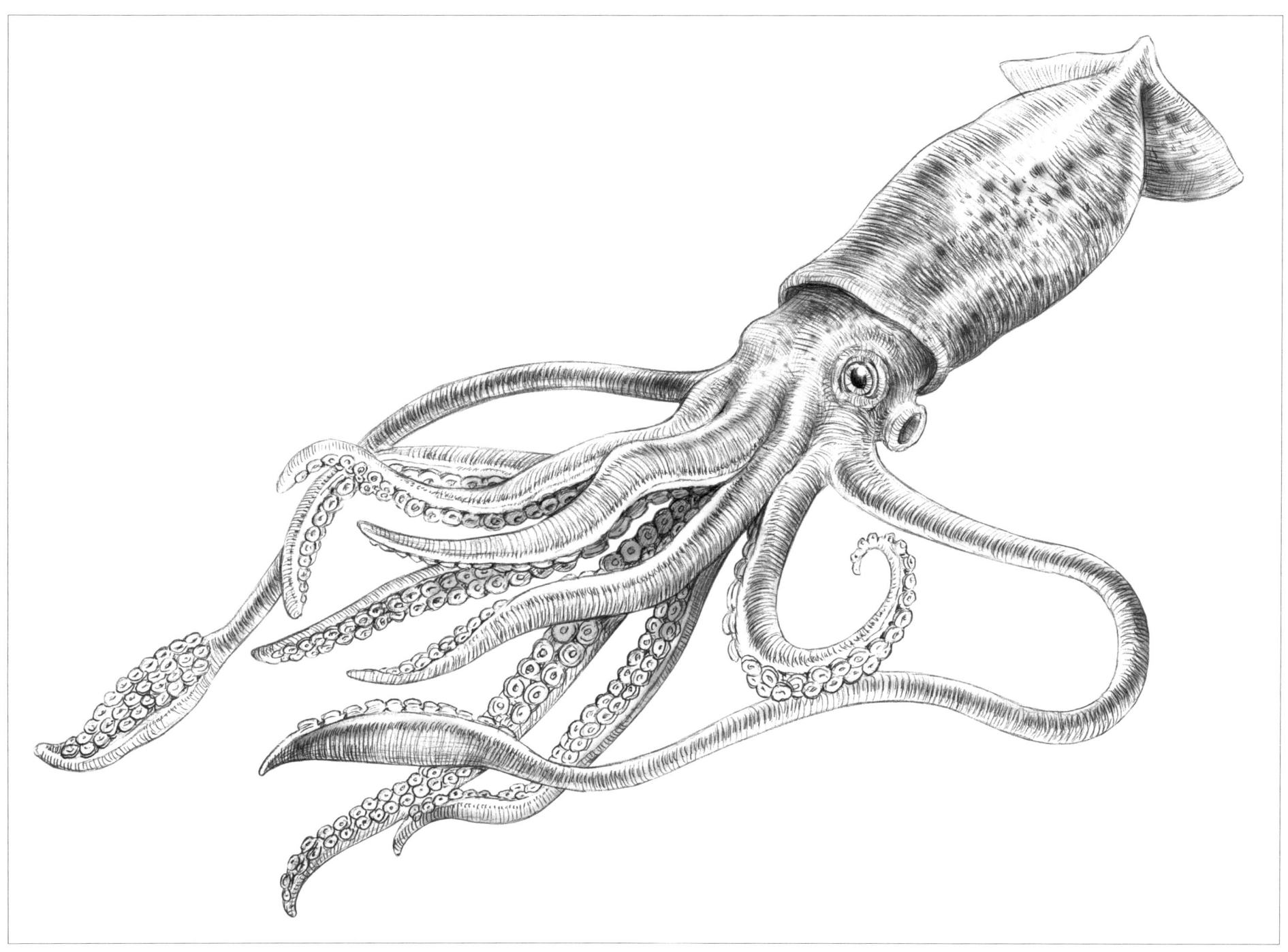

Giant Squid

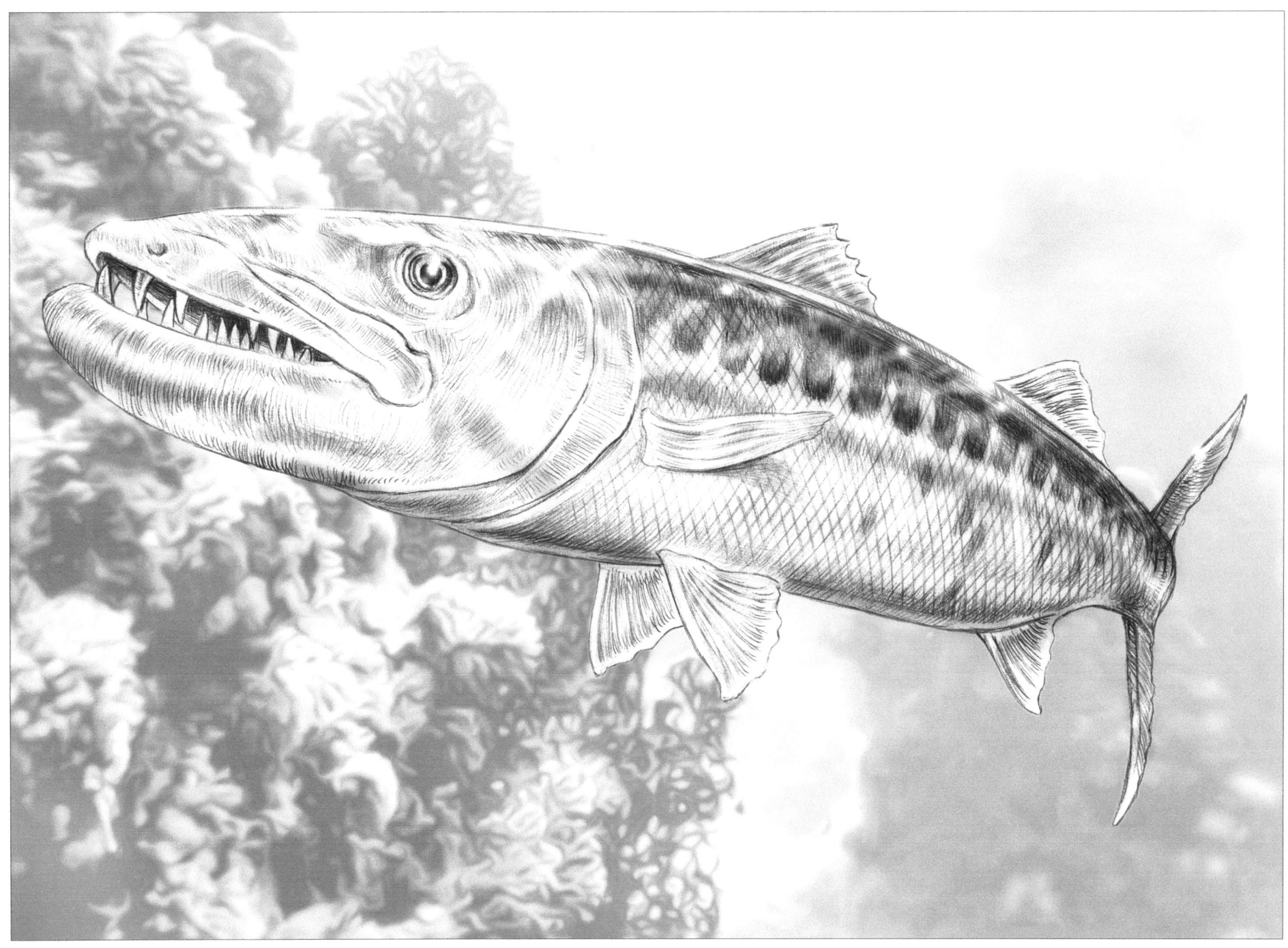

Great Barracuda

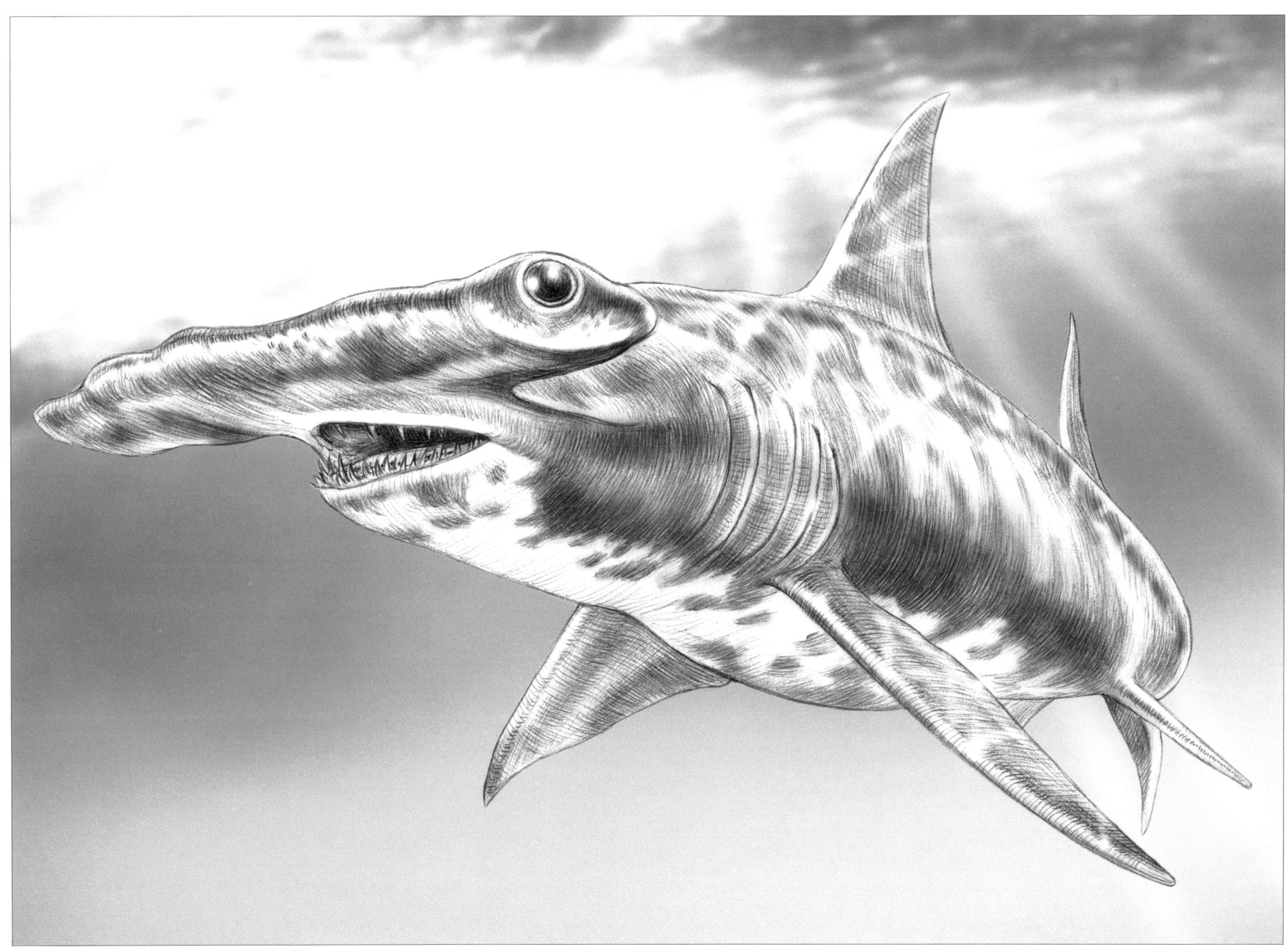

Great Hammerhead Shark

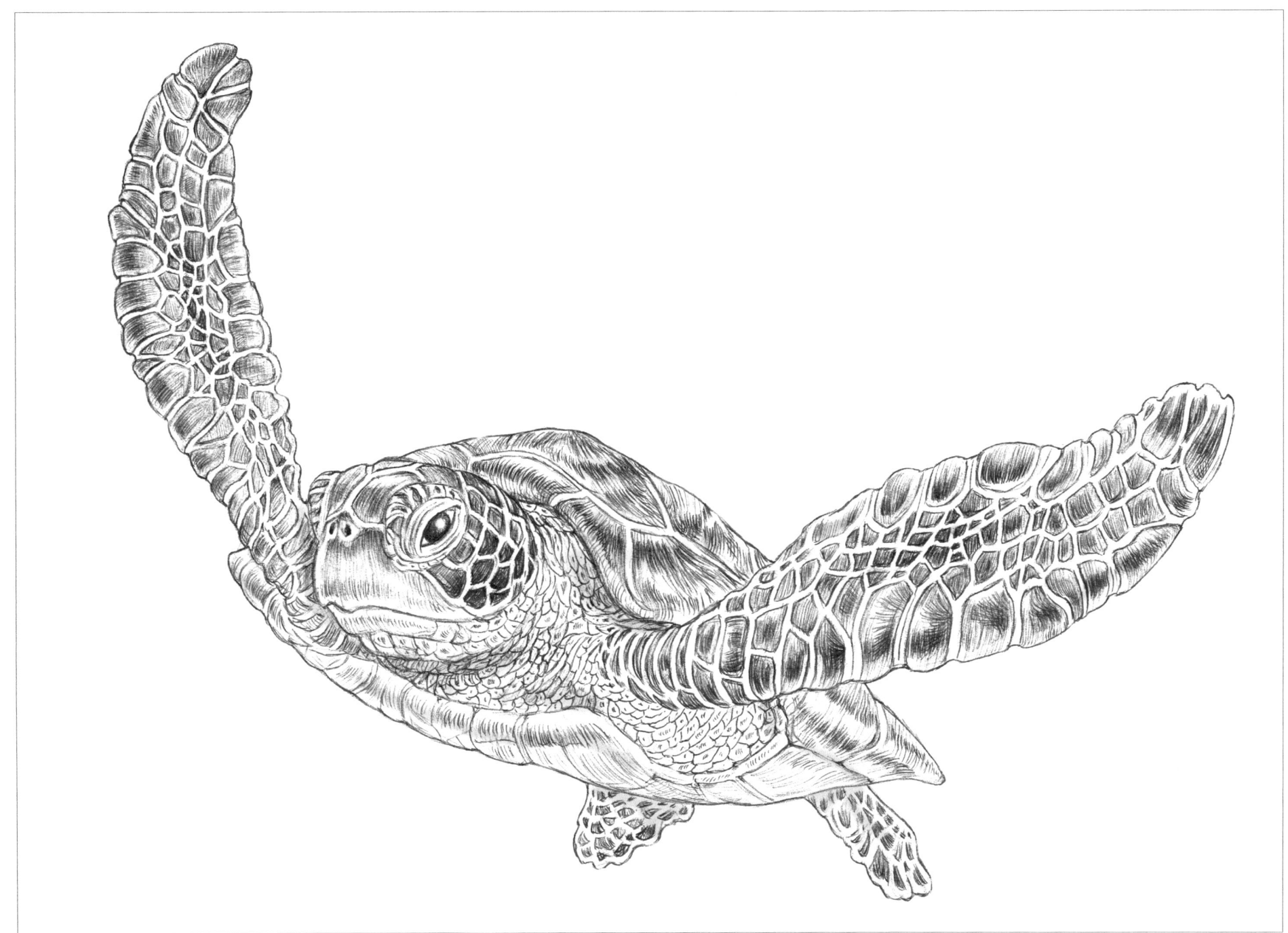

Hawksbill Sea Turtle

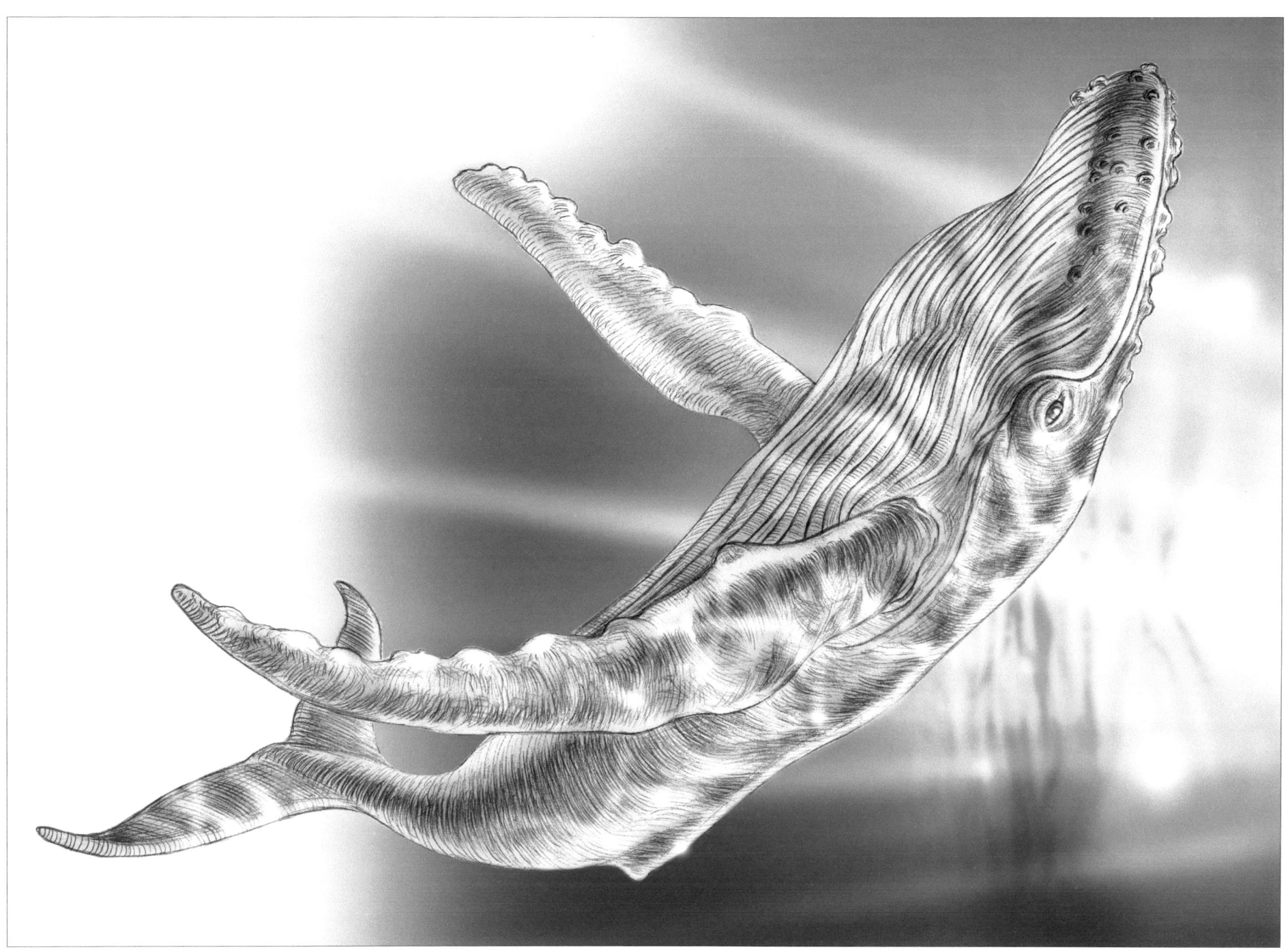

Humpback Whale

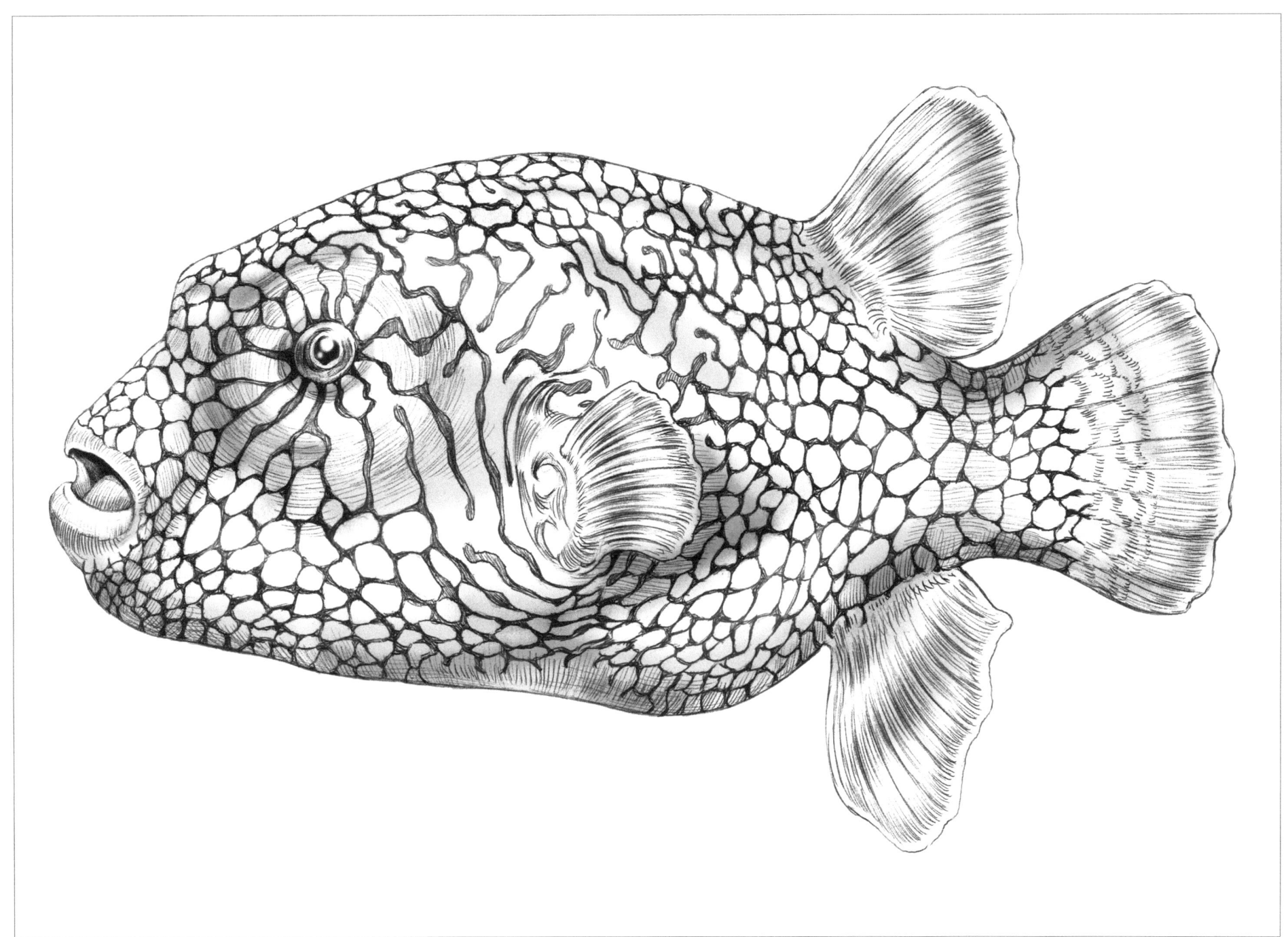

Map Pufferfish

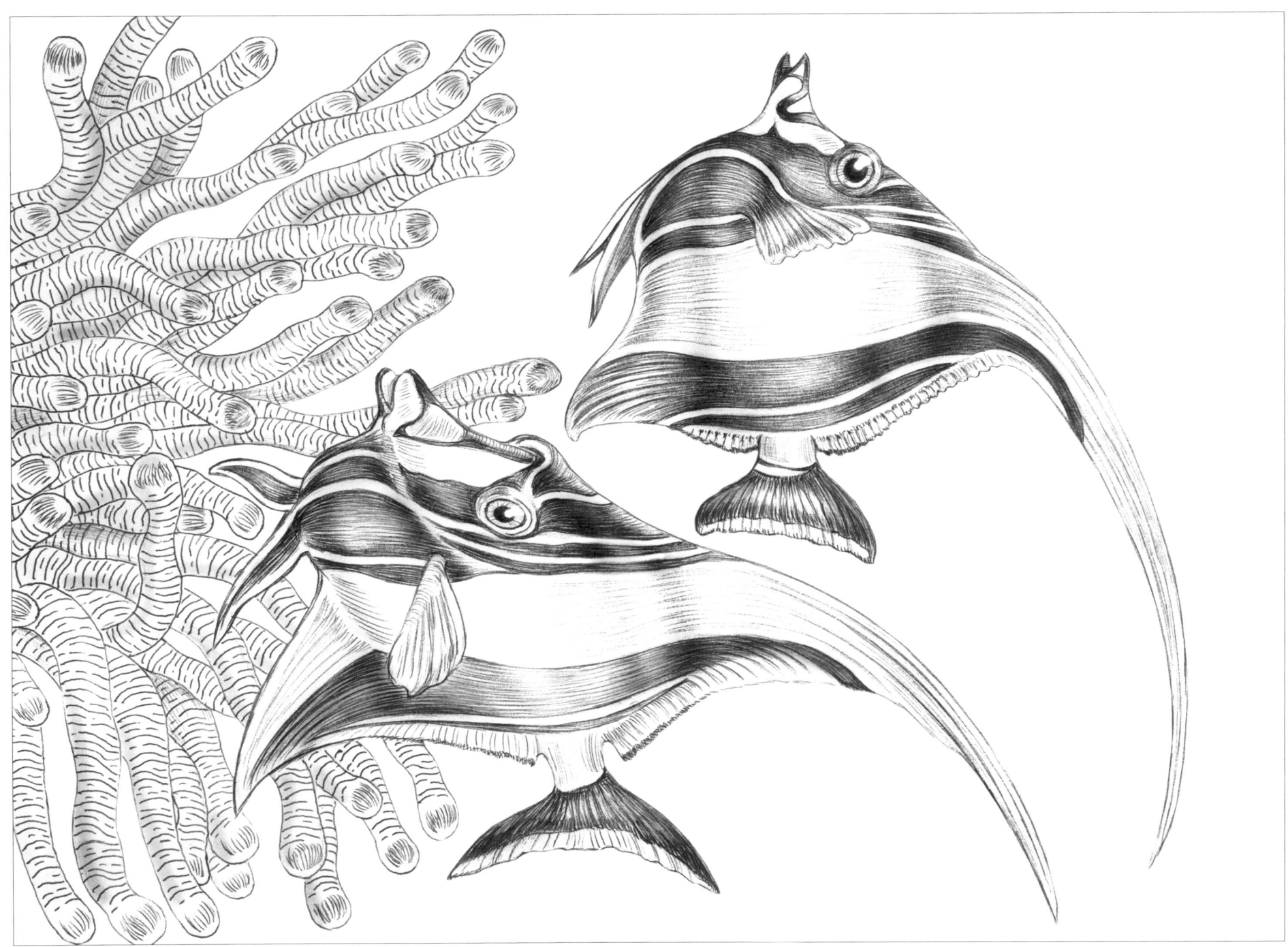

Moorish Idol

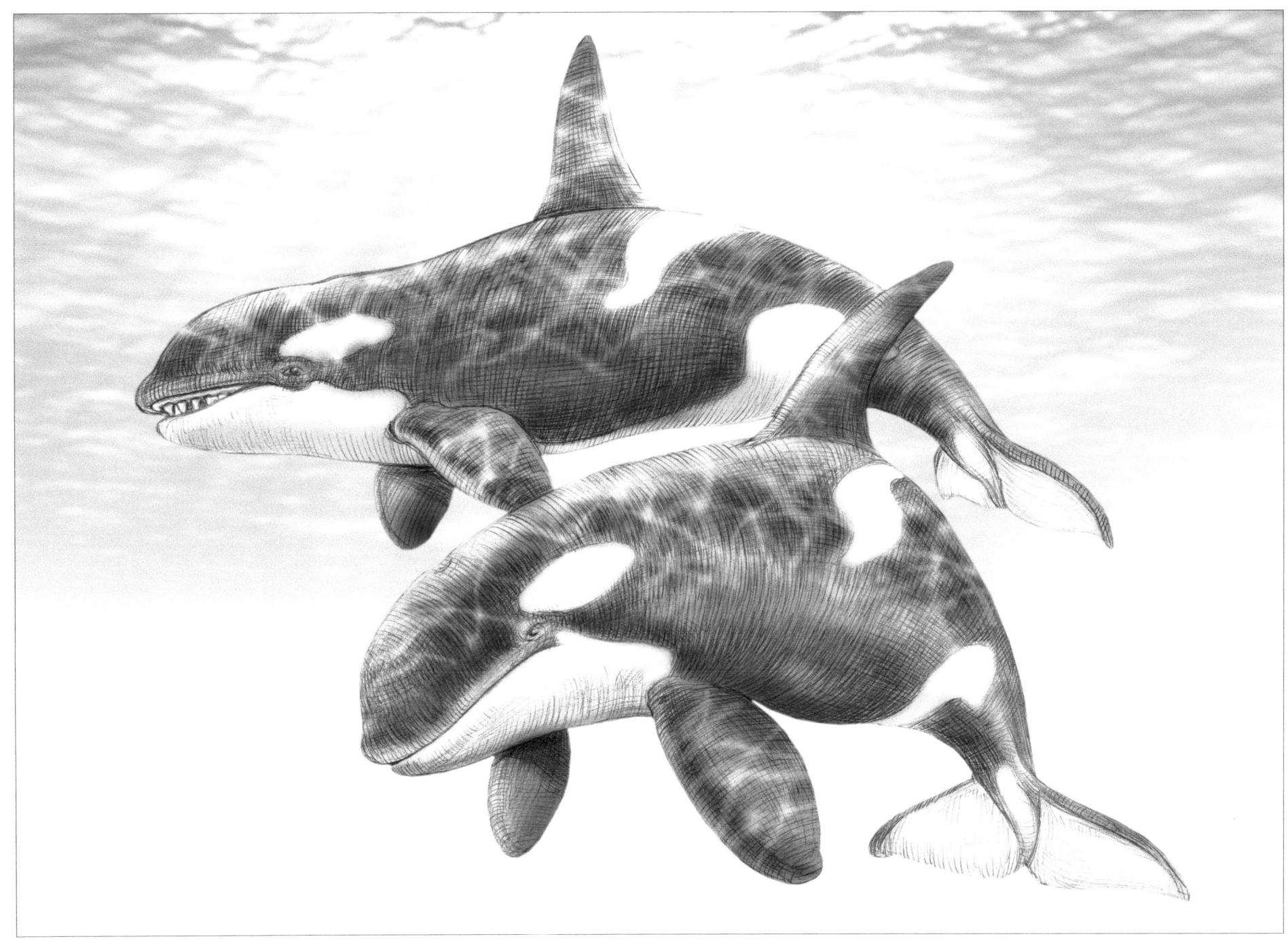
Orcas

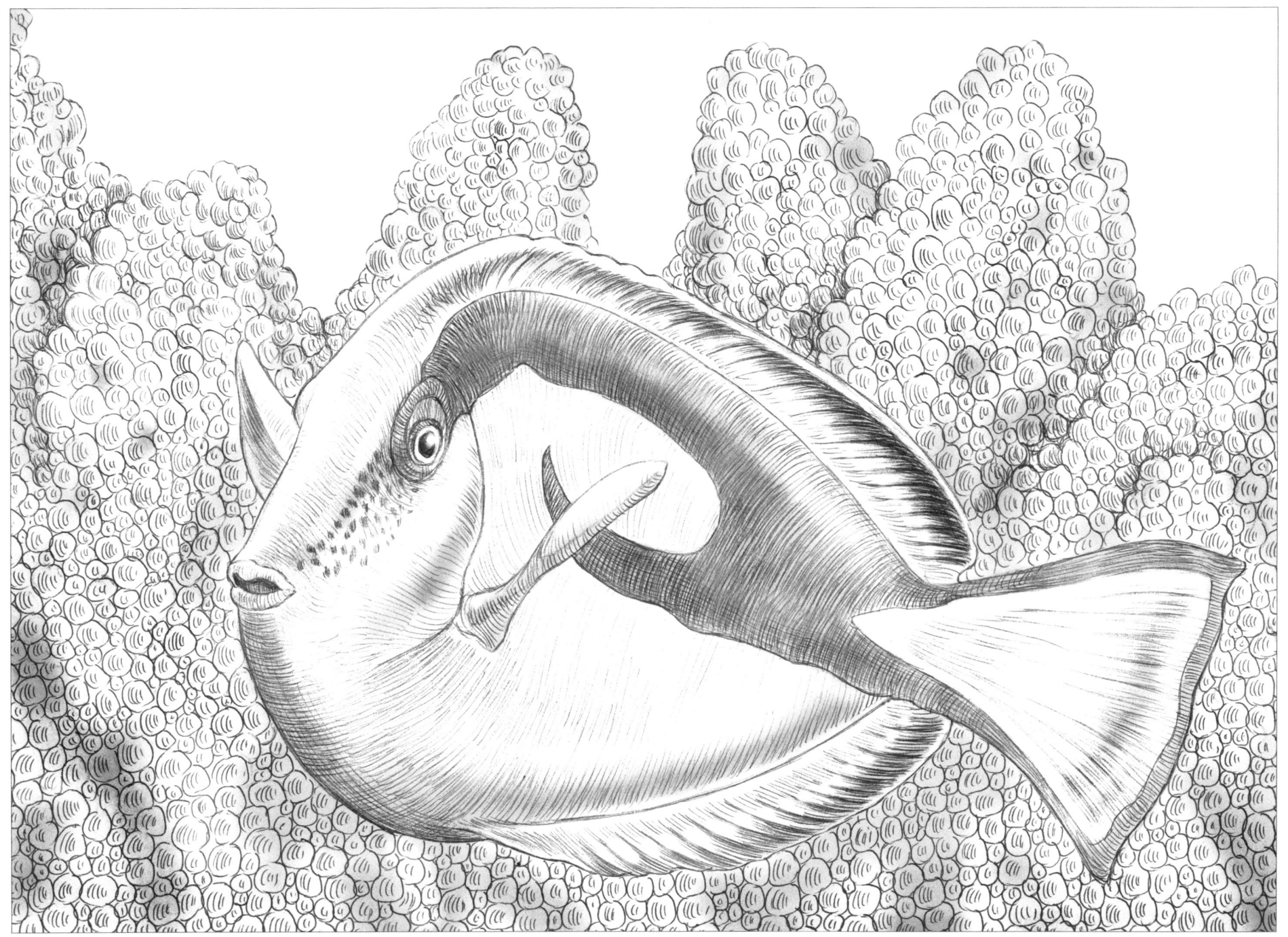

Regal Blue Tang

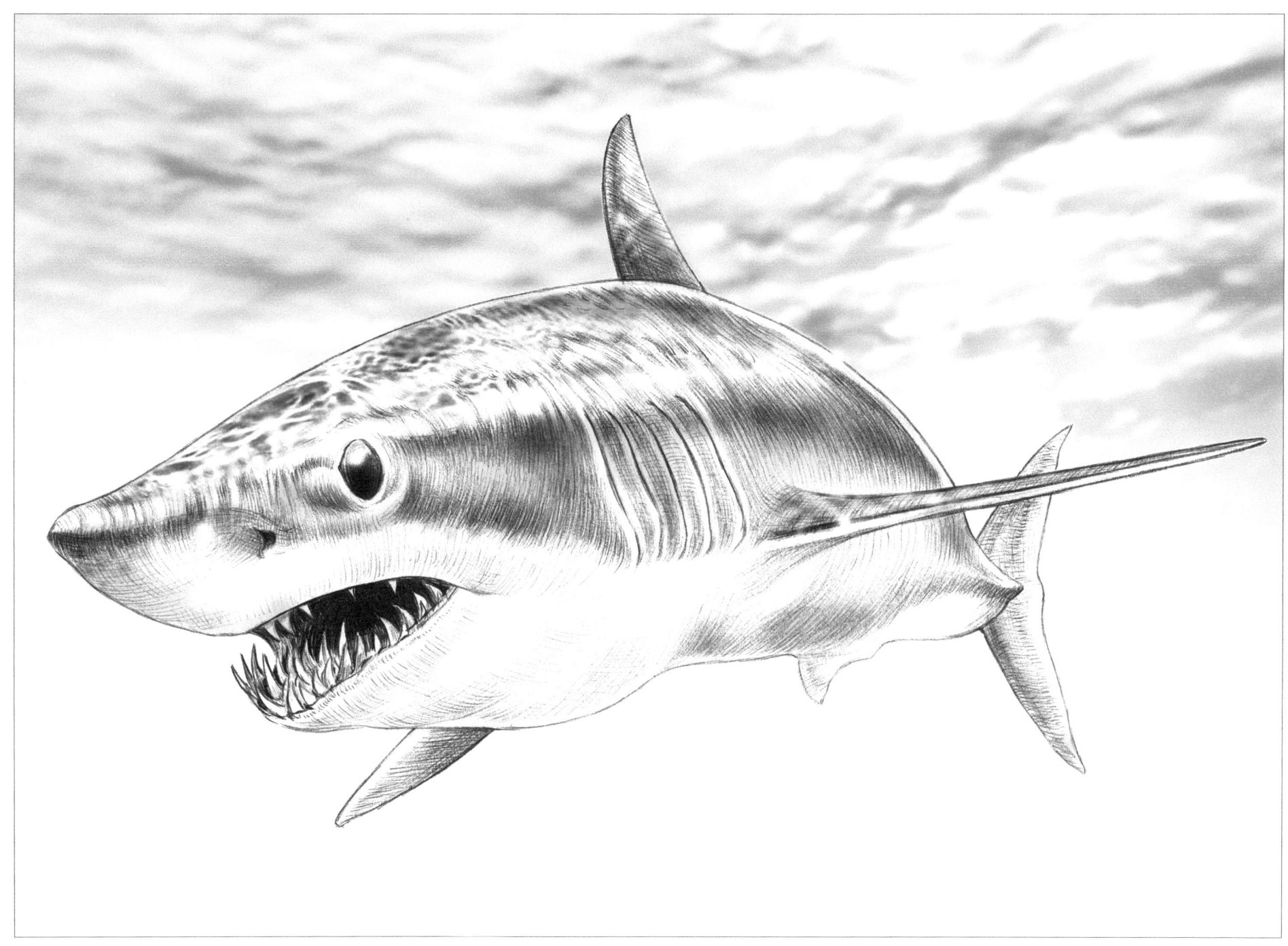

Shortfin Mako Shark

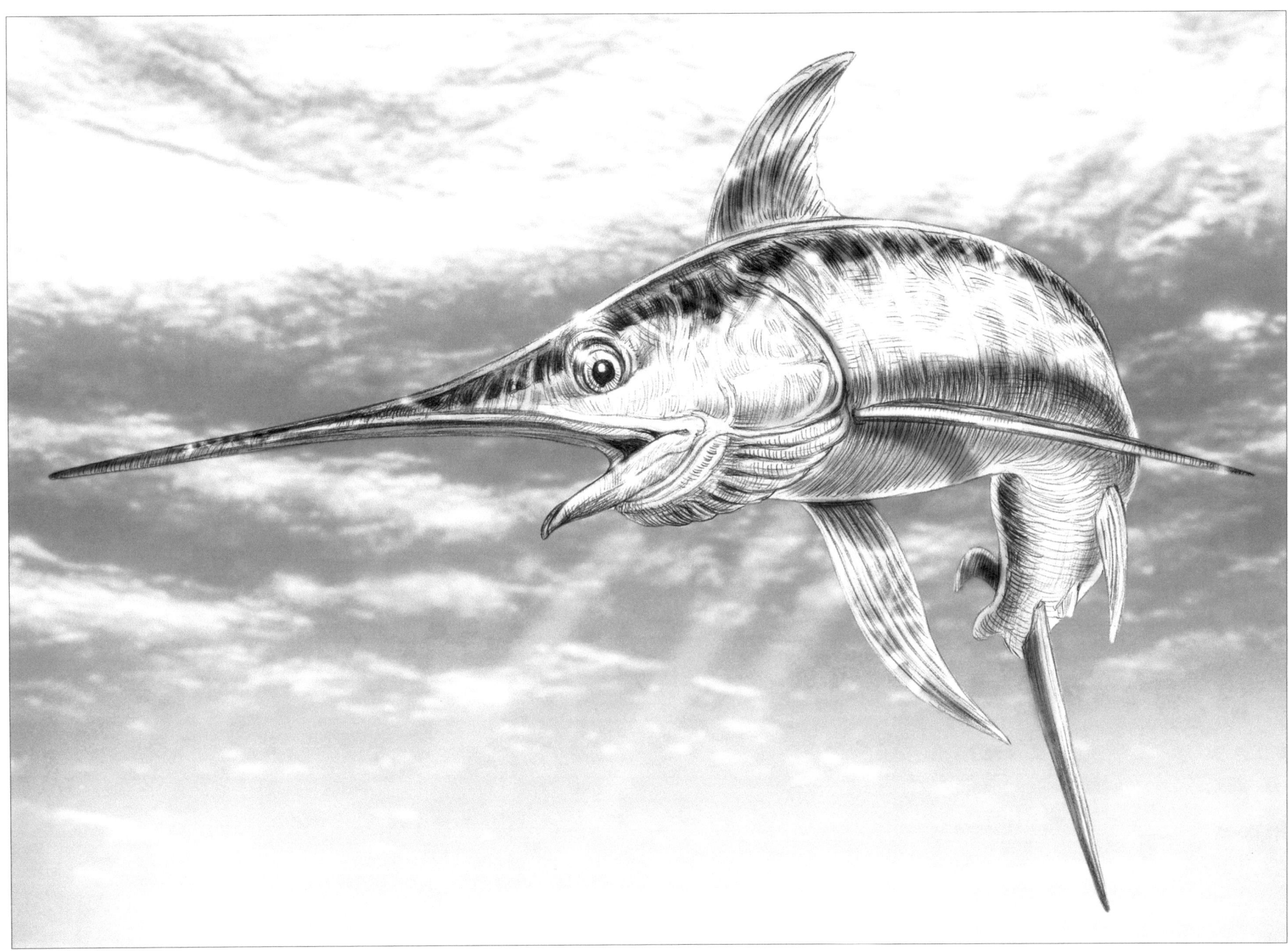

Swordfish

Tim Jeffs is a New York City based artist and illustrator who has been creating dynamic artwork for over 25 years. Animals are a favorite subject matter of his, along with the complex and intricate details these creatures possess. *"The incredible diversity and complexity of animals has always intrigued me. They offer endless pleasure to look and marvel upon. In every drawing I try to capture the unique quality of each particular animal. I hope you enjoy my perspective, love and admiration of these incredible creatures."*

Visit my website for prints, digital coloring books and coloring lessons:

www.TimJeffsArt.com

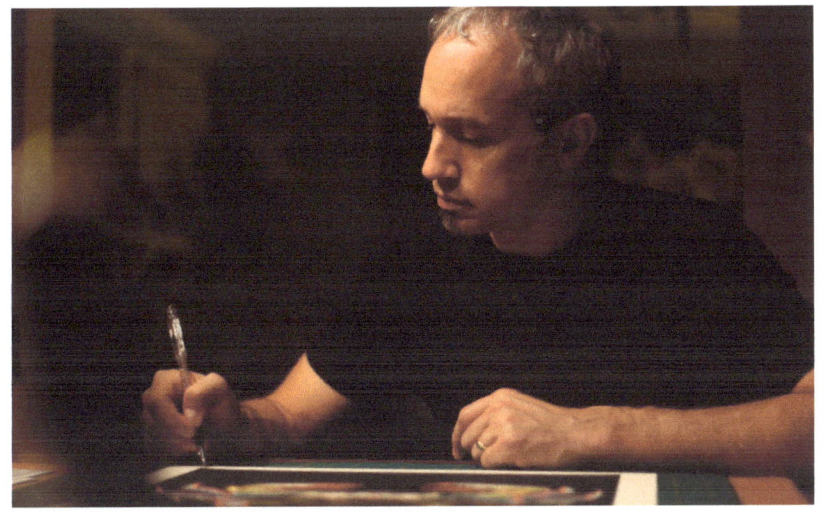

Discover the full line of Tim Jeffs' Published Coloring Books

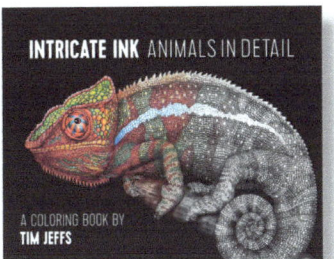 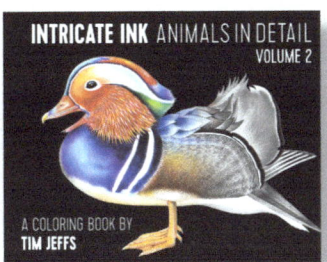 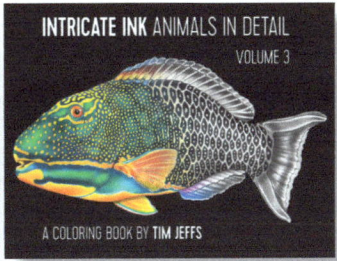 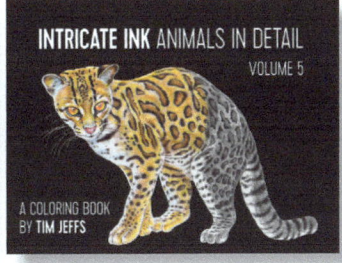 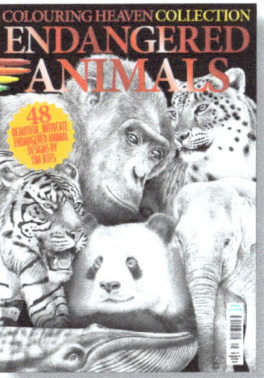

Intricate Ink Animals In Detail Volume 1, 2 3 and 5 Available at:
Pomegranate.com
Amazon.com
Bookdepository.com

**Colouring Heaven Collection
Endangered Animals**
Available at: Colouringheaven.com

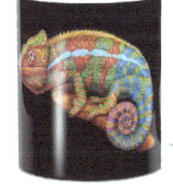

Discover Tim Jeffs' Merchandise

Etsy Shop
www.etsy.com/shop/TimJeffsArt

Society6 Shop
www.society6.com/TimJeffsArt

Redbubble Shop
TimJeffsArt.redbubble.com

Vsual Print Shop
https://vsual.co/shop/tim-jeffs-art

Discover the full line of Tim Jeffs Digital Coloring Books at:
www.TimJeffsArt.com

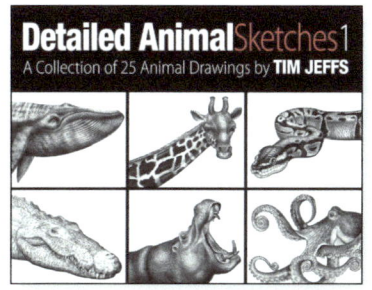
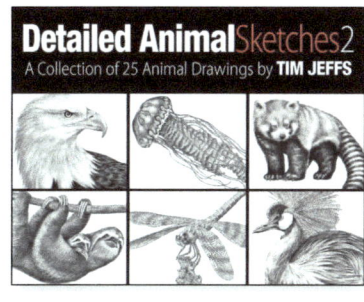
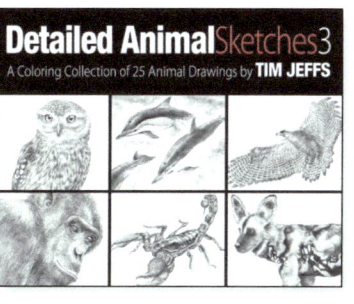
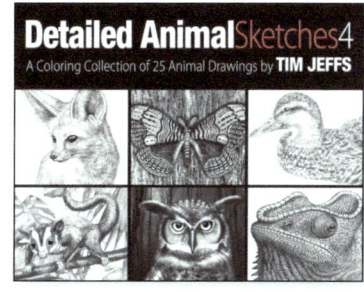
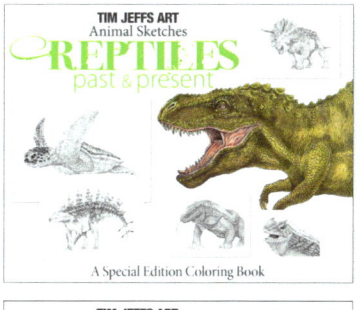

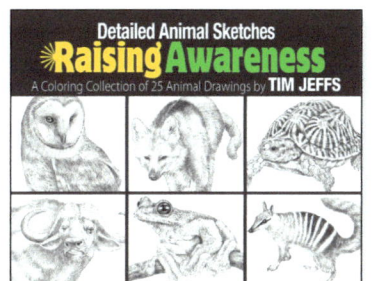
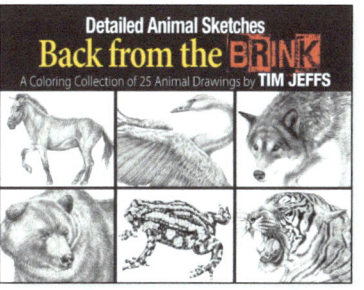
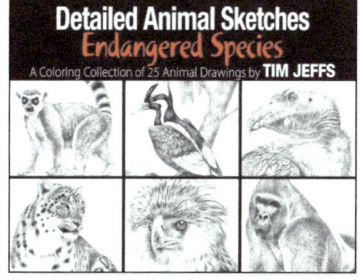
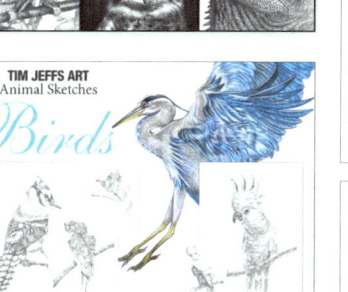
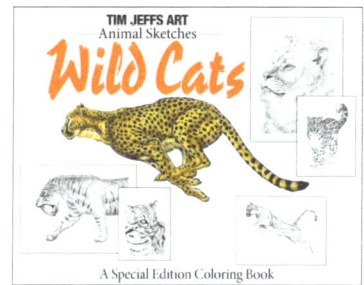

And Coloring Lessons

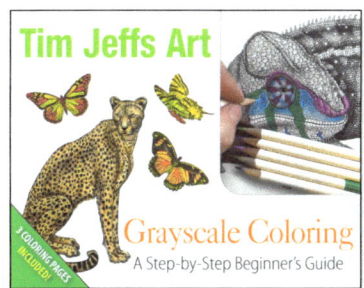
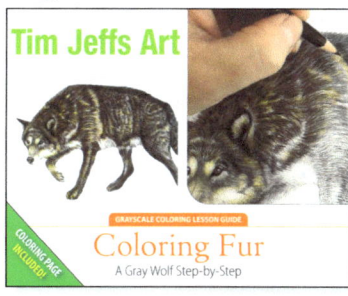
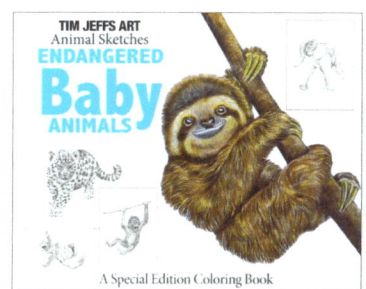

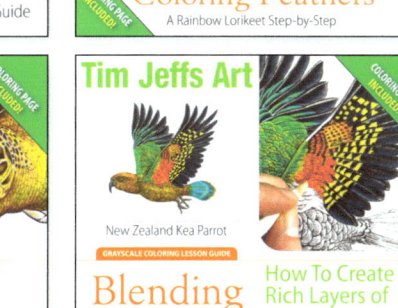
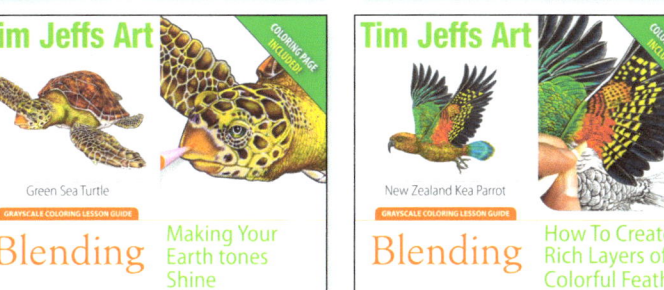
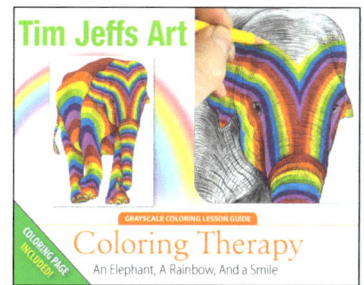
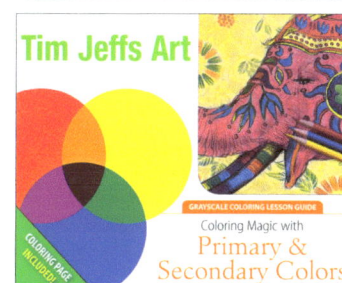
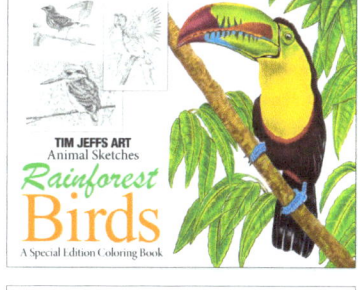
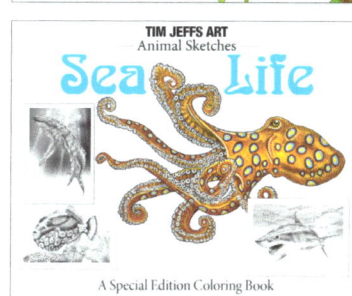
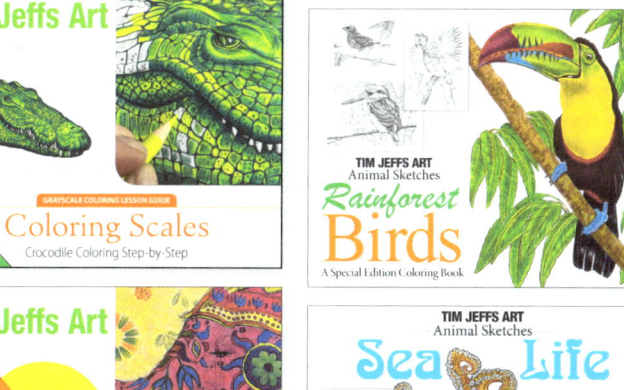
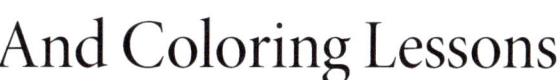

TIM JEFFS ART Online Resources

Share Your Creativity with the World!

Join the ever-expanding coloring group of animal lovers who inspire each other through their colorings of the animals from Tim's books and lessons. With thousands of members from all around the world, Tim's Facebook group "Intricate Ink Coloring Group" is a creative and safe space where everyone is welcome. Jo Warren, the groups all-inspiring administrator will welcome you in with open arms and is there to encourage everyone to just have fun no matter your coloring skill level. Come join, we can't wait to have you as a member! Join Tim's Facebook Coloring Group at:

www.facebook.com/groups/intricateink

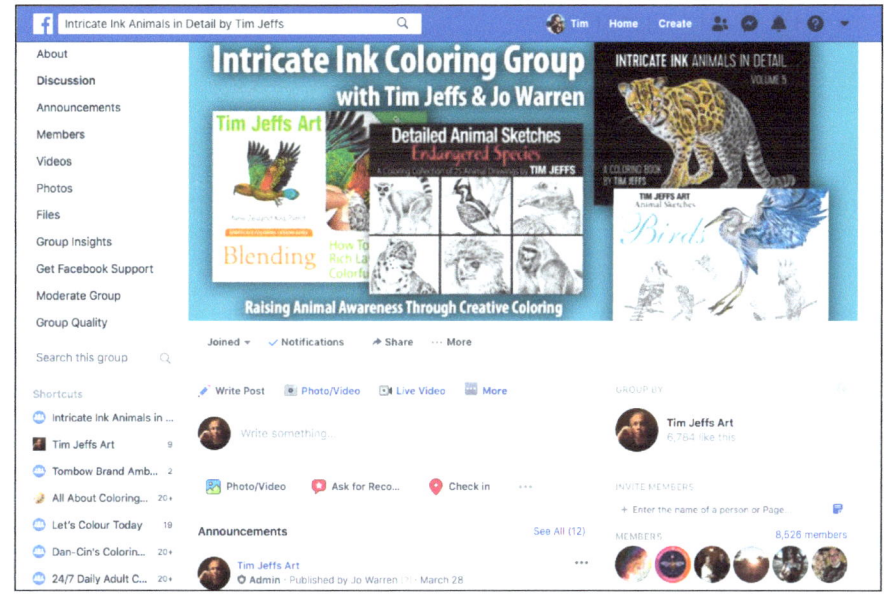

Visit the Home of Tim Jeffs Art

TimJeffsArt.com is my home on the web where I display all of my work and various projects. I hope you can stop by for a visit! You'll find my new shop where signed and unsigned prints of all of my animal drawings are available to purchase, along with the complete library of my digital download coloring books and grayscale coloring lessons. In the conservation section, you can see the projects that I am very proud of. Using my art to preserve wildlife is so important to me.

www.TimJeffsArt.com

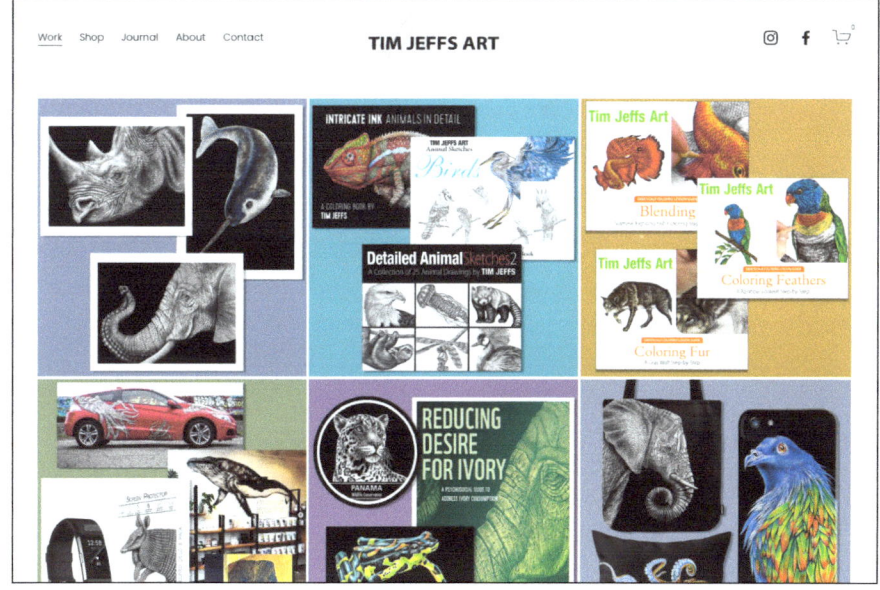